so Far so GOOD

MARIATI YAHYA

PARTRIDGE
A Penguin Random House Company

To order additional copies of this book, contact
Toll Free 800 101 2657 (Singapore)
Toll Free 1 800 81 7340 (Malaysia)
orders.singapore@partridgepublishing.com

www.partridgepublishing.com/singapore

CONTENTS

DEDICATION

This book is dedicated to all retirees.

Although you have not reached your destination,
you should continue your journey
because now you know which turn to take.

ACKNOWLEDGEMENT

Thank you to all who have given me endless encouragement, motivation and financial support to make this dream of writing my first book a reality. Special thanks to Nadia Muliadi, my niece from Canada for her tireless effort to proofread and edit my manuscript. Not forgetting my dear mother for her patience and dedication.

PREFACE

Writing a book on retirement was an idea sprung from the challenge of transitioning from one lifestyle to another.

I've been holding on to a dusty and aging bucket list of ideas tucked deep in the corners of my mind and writing a book is one of them.

The decision was made 20 years ago before I decided to retire in 2009.

Perhaps it is the fear of change. We tend to give excuses, always putting things off. I owe it to myself to go ahead, gain new experiences and start making this project a reality.

So why didn't I start writing immediately after my retirement? Why now? Like retirement, writing a book takes time and planning. I hung around for a while to see what worked and what didn't. I wanted to make sure that this book will be filled with true, unique experiences that reflect my value and personality.

There are tons of books out there that will tell you how to financially plan your retirement. Financial independence doesn't only mean in dollars and cents, it's also independence from what's been weighing us down throughout our working life.

So is retirement on a shoestring possible? You've got to dig deep into this book to find out.

This is never about learning how to earn millions on retiring. Because everyone is different, I should only tell you about my experiences during my 3 years into retirement; about what works and what doesn't for me and some advice on equipping yourself financially to face the glaring stare of retirement.

Perhaps you might learn something from this book. All of your efforts will be worth it.

Now I'm off to spring clean and bring forth my ideas off this bucket list.

Happy reading.

Mariati Yahya

INTRODUCTION

Since my retirement in 2009, I have been writing my journal religiously on Facebook. I'm quite happy with the feedback and response I've been getting. Once in a while, my friends will call to find out how I'm getting along with my retirement. This spurred me to write even more.

While people have been concerned about my coping with retirement with no steady income to see me through old age, I believe that it's still possible to do one's best. This is certainly not the preferred lifestyle for those who are used to finding their identity through work. I've been there and have emerged unscathed so far.

Now for those who've been curious to know about my progress, here's a book I've written for you.

There is a strong link between money and retirement. Even if you're not retired, money will always be a necessity. Nothing is for free. How you embrace your lifestyle depends on how much you are worth monetarily.

While there are so many ways to plan your retirement, you may already have one or two things up your sleeve.

Dare yourself to see it through. Keep doing your thing. You must break free from the chorus in order to discover the sound of your own voice.

As I aim to lead a simple life, let me share with you some of my tips on generating income that's sustainable enough to get by.

However, this book is not to educate or discuss the issue of the big F word—Finance. I'm focusing on only the positive aspects of retirement. My retirement, specifically.

If you're able to learn something from this book, then you've made my sharing effort worthwhile.

As this is my first attempt at writing a book, I'll be keeping it concise. I hope you'll also like the sketches I included; they've always been a source of amusement for me.

And who knows perhaps there might be an alternative version of So Far So Good in the works that's made up entirely of sketches.

TAKING THE PLUNGE

Many people look forward to retiring with great anticipation and anxiety. When you've reached a certain age, along with other factors in tow, you just know when it's time.

I've risen through the ranks with hard work and building good rapport with my bosses and colleagues. I've also been constantly improving my educational status by taking up relevant in-house and external courses.

But after nearly forty years working in the civil service, my gut feeling is telling me enough is enough. No doubt having a job helps to pay the bills but it isn't stimulating anymore. I need to engage my soul's desire for something new.

I wouldn't mind leaving the rat race with less cheese. What's more important is my happiness, and improving the quality of my life.

So during this reorientation phase, I find myself asking these questions:

- What's missing? What do I need to do to find the missing link?
- What do I enjoy doing but never had the chance to?
- What can I do with my talents and interests?
- What do I regret not doing in my life? Would I have to dig deeper into my pocket?
- How can I offer my skills and talents while being my own boss?
- Do I need to venture out?

This isn't the end of my list. The more I look at it, the more I realise the need to re-prioritise. I did extend my employment for a further six months after my retirement period. Here are the following reasons I decided to call it quits:

Burnout Leads to Boredom

It could happen to anyone without them realising. It's a gradual process over a long period of time. Work-related stress isn't the only reason; other factors including lifestyle choices and individual personality traits could also be the contributing factors of burnout.

As for me, the main reason is my job. Working at the same place and doing the same job repeatedly over the years has its drawbacks. It's becoming unbearably routine and stressful for me, leaving me with little or no motivation and the sense of emptiness. As a result, my productivity efforts are affected.

As if to rub salt into the wound, some may find that there's a common practice of leaving older workers out on future career advancements and project works that usually comes with a chance of promotion. The office bullying, the rampant politicking and so on are becoming sure signs of stress and burnout.

If I may throw in my two cents worth, watch out for some of the following signs for burnout:

- Every day's a Monday and getting out of bed for work takes Herculean effort.
- Calling in sick every other day except when your favourite doctor goes on holiday.
- Being awarded as the MC King/Queen, putting the Academy Awards to shame.
- You're always feeling exhausted at work.
- Your work's no longer challenging or interesting but monotonous and overwhelming.
- You're cynical and resentful all the time for no apparent reason.
- Demanding job expectations.
- Lack of recognition.
- You get annoyed by your immediate supervisor or boss.
- You feel you're only working for the money and a bonus is the only thing you're expecting at the end of the year.

Wish I had recognised the warning signs of impending burnout earlier so I could take steps to getting my work life back on track. Anyway, the fire in the belly has gone out.

Taking Care and Bonding Time with Aged Parent

Being a single parent taking care of thirteen children is a mighty achievement second only to the greatness of God. I was a witness to this while growing up and it's not easy. I'm talking about my mother, the super woman who's now in her eighties.

This is one of the facets of retirement I always look forward to fulfilling: that is to spend more time with my mother.

I'm glad I don't belong to the "sandwich generation", a term usually associated with baby boomers even though I was born during that period between 1946 and 1964. These are the people who are caring for and supporting their aging parents and families of their own while managing a career and funding for their retirement. Being single, however, makes it easier for me.

I'm also lucky to have my siblings helping me with taking care of my mother's well-being, financial and emotional needs. And now, taking up the new role of a full-time caregiver, daughter and companion will only make me a stronger person in many aspects of my life.

It's time to give back.

Spiritual Needs

Work's taking most of my time, leaving me little of it to pursue other interests. Doing what is required of me to practice my faith is expected. The concept of spirituality varies between people and their beliefs. As I am into my sunset years, the need to better myself spiritually holds more importance than everything else. I need something conducive to my current situation to acquire more spiritual knowledge and become a better person in the process.

Since work is taking a toll on my mental and physical health, it's high time I take my leave.

Financial Independence

The key to achieving an active and satisfying retirement involves more than looking at your financial needs. You don't need a million dollars to have a great retirement. It is having enough to live the rest of your life the way you want it to be.

Don't make the mistake of thinking you can't have million dollars or you'll never be able to retire. Don't get trapped into thinking that bad economic conditions mean a lifetime of financial misery.

So is retiring on a shoestring possible?

Knowing that I have some substantial financial account with CPF upon retiring and having special retirement account that

I've created and maintained since twenty years ago, plus my own savings accounts, I think I can manage.

In addition to changing and adapting to a new lifestyle, I can downgrade to a smaller house with the proceeds of the sale going into my coffer. Of course I'm not planning on doing nothing afterward. I'll start doing the things I love doing and using my God-given talents to keep the income flowing in.

As long as I put my money in a proper perspective, I don't need a million dollars to retire.

By taking a bold step to initiate retirement, I hope it's payback time for the many aspects of life that I missed. I'm ready to claim my freedom from being an employee to being the boss at my own time.

God willing, I'll make it.

THIS BOOK WILL BE FILLED WITH TRUE, UNIQUE EXPERIENCES THAT REFLECT MY VALUES AND PERSONALITIES

......SAVING IS A GOOD HABIT WORTH CONTINUING EVEN
DURING YOUR RETIREMENT. PUT YOUR MONEY IN PROPER
PERSPECTIVE AND YOU ARE GOOD TO GO

SAYING GOODBYE IS NOT EASY

The following is an extract and part of my farewell email to my colleagues:

Dear friends,

This coming Friday (21.8.09) marks the last day of my service as an employee and the beginning of my next phase in life as a retiree.

I have served my employer as a civil servant for 40 years (37 years, plus a few years in a private company)! Phew! Most of you weren't even born yet or some were still toddlers learning how to walk.

So on my last day, I'd like to share with you my 37 years of good times. Yes, only the good times. Why should I be talking about the bad times on my last day?

I'd like to take you back to a time when I was still working at the Fullerton Building.

Before this, I was working with another government department. I asked for a transfer after working with them for about 9 years.

"We got good news and bad news for you," they said. "The good news is your request for transfer is approved. The bad news is you're going to . . ."

So do you see how our reputation has grown compared to then? I have no regrets coming here.

Working in Fullerton Building was quite an adventure. We didn't have that many computers but heaps of files, index cards and dusty ceiling fans whirling tirelessly over our heads. Once in a while, you'll hear little sounds from mice scampering around and teasing us. Birds would occasionally come to visit us although they almost never found an exit. We'd always have to shoo them away and lead the way out.

When we had to retrieve files, we had to visit the basement. We'd usually go in groups because the basement was dark and quite eerie. Did you know that the Fullerton Building used to house prisoners during the Japanese Occupation? We heard lots of eerie stories from the watchman.

When it was time for us to move to a new building, we found ourselves moving along with the advancement of technology as well. From doing clerical duties, I adapted with the changes and became more 'technical'. My journey up was a long and winding road, making me wiser. It became life of my years instead of the years of my life.

The most valuable gift is the gift of friendship that I acquired throughout my working life here. Some of my colleagues called me *kakak* which means big sister. It's been an honour!

I'd like to give my thanks to the many *sifus* whom I owe my experience and knowledge gain to. You all know who you are.

Soon I won't have to 'sleepwalk' my way to the restrooms. I will miss rushing for the bus and the train. However I'm proud to say that amidst all the rushing, I've learned to perfect the technique of slithering my way in and out of the crowded train with ease!

And on the way home I will also miss being the polite lady who always looks down in the crowded train because of the wave of excruciating bodily aromas. You know my height is around armpit level so can't help but to look down all the way home!

Wow. There are lots to talk about but only a few lines left. You must be wondering what my plans are. Well, I'm going to have a very long and deserving rest doing absolutely nothing and . . .

Thank you for the lovely cards, presents and also for the wonderful lunch and dinner treats.

I don't believe in goodbyes. So see you around because we are, after all, in this little red dot. We will meet. No one grows old by living but grows old by losing interest in living.

My journey continues.

Now the candle is burning at both ends
It will not last the night
But my dear friends
It has given me the loveliest & brightest of light

Thank you.

I AM READY TO CLAIM MY FREEDOM FROM BEING AN EMPLOYEE TO BEING THE BOSS OF MY OWN TIME

WHAT I MISSED ABOUT WORK IS COMING HOME IN
A CROWDED TRAIN....

TICKLE–TICKLE LITTLE STUFF

- Goodbye, tension. Hello, passion.
- Your experiences don't age when you retire; they get younger.
- You discover that rainbows have more than seven colours. You are the eighth!
- Since retirement, you've long forgotten there's such a thing called an alarm clock.
- Monday blues are for when you're working. Monday blooms are for when you're retired.
- Another word for retire is 're-tyre'. You're changing tyres to proceed with your journey, fully charged.
- Staying at home during retirement is like going on a staycation. You have all the time in the world to discover anything and everything within yourself, around the house, your neighbourhood and more.
- Money is enough if you put them in proper perspective. Remember saving is a good habit. The more the better.

- Although you haven't reached your destination, you should continue your journey because you now know which turn to take.
- RETIRE is not a sick letter-words it is a healthy word.
- Cut and paste was an 'awful-cial' thing to do then, but an artful thing to do now.
- You used to laugh at your boss' cynical jokes. Now you have time to acquire a new language that teaches you how to laugh in different ways: LOL, ROFL, LMAO . . .
- My motto for not continuing working after retirement: Left is always Right.
- Work gives you money; retirement gives you honey.
- You are as busy as a bee when you're working but a bird freed from its cage when you're retired.
- It used to be book-keeping for measure. Now it's keeping books for pleasure.
- You used to take orders all the time. Now you place orders all the time.
- You used to be told to do this and that or you'll be out of work. Now doing this and that is just a workout.
- Dates are supposed to be sweet; the only known bitter dates are called dateline.
- Inspire yourself with new insight.
- When you are retired, you become your full-time job.
- Retired from something but living for a multitude of things.
- When work gives you lemons you don't have to make lemonades. When retirement gives you time, make it chime for you'll need it in your prime.

- Resting is not idling, doing nothing is not procrastinating, day dreaming is sleeping with an open mind and goofing around is 'jestifying'. In retirement, I call it negative positivity. It works!
- If punishment is a reward for a lifetime of hard work then it's for the uninspired. You've got to live and believe.
- Been there, done that. So what's next?
- You are not over the hill when you're retired. You still need to conquer more. Take baby steps. Time is at your side.
- Then again it's okay to be on top or over the hill as long as you are young at heart and healthy rather than being under the hill because then, life has ceased.
- So what if you are in your sixties? Age is not important here unless you are a cheese or a vintage wine. In fact they are sought after.
- Every morning used to be a dawn of a new error. Now morning is the dawn of a new scorer. Score in life.
- In retirement, you have to exercise your mind regularly. Otherwise your mentality will remain at room temperature.

TO STAY HEALTHY LONG INTO YOUR GOLDEN YEARS MAKE
THE DOCTOR YOUR NEW BEST FRIEND BY VISITING HIM OR
HER REGULARLY FOR MEDICAL CHECK-UPS AND TEST

THE BUCKET LIST

Having a bucket list can help you turn your dreams into reality after retirement. With work out of your mind, you don't want your days passing by without any productivity.

It's different than having a To-Do-List which is framed within a certain social context. The bucket list, on the other hand, opens up the context. It's a platform to set anything and everything you've ever wanted to do—be it random, big, or small.

Everyone measures time similarly but experiences it subjectively. This is why having a bucket list is ideal because it maximises the opportunity to live your dreams to the fullest.

You can update it as you please, add or subtract your list and make choices with it. Rather than engaging our time in pointless activities, we are directing it fully toward what matters most to us.

After 20 years, my bucket list is still a work-in-progress. Still it gives me something to strive for. I keep adding, changing and updating it to suit my needs and situation.

The following are some of the things I would like to do and achieve during my retirement:

1. Continue saving for my retirement as and when there's an income
2. Continue to go on vacation for as long as I can afford
3. Write a book or more books
4. Enroll in courses or continue to further my studies
5. Do small business
6. Teach
7. Volunteer
8. Sell my art pieces
9. Meet more people/ renew friendship with friends and relatives
10. Ride a bicycle
11. Attend to my spiritual needs
12. Keep up with the latest technology
13. Stay healthy
14. Turn the extra room into an art studio/home office

Writing this bucket list has been an incredible insightful exercise. It's giving new meaning to my enthusiasm knowing what's in store ahead.

To discover details of how I am living my dream, please read the chapter on So Far So Good.

THE SPORT STADIUM IS JUST A WALKING DISTANCE FROM
WHERE I LIVED. SO EVERYDAY AFTER MY MORNING PRAYERS, I
WILL GO THERE TO DO TAI CHI, JOGGING AD SOCIALISING

YOU ALWAYS HEAR STUDENTS DROPPING OUT OF SCHOOL BUT AS FOR ME, I AM PROUD TO SAY THAT I HAVE DROPPED IN

SO FAR SO GOOD

After three years into retirement, I've got into the groove of doing things in a leisurely pace without guilt.

Retirees who are used to having a busy lifestyle may feel that having too much time on their hands can lead to boredom. The best way to overcome this is to do something you love; be it going back to school, learning something new, vacations, volunteer work, writing a book, or spending quality time with old friends and relatives.

It's time to reactivate those hobbies you've put aside for so many years. Who knows what good will come out of it?

By giving yourself the chance, you might be able to earn some income while doing something you truly love.

Don't let your new-found freedom be boring and unfulfilling. You have all the time and opportunity to develop yourself in so many ways. Inspire yourself with some new insight. However without action your new found insight is useless.

Most importantly, let in some laughter in your life. Humour lets you see things from a different perspective. This book is sprinkled with light-hearted funnies in the form of sketches of my daily life.

So are you now looking forward to retiring? Perhaps you're still looking around to see what's in store for you.

If you're still curious, here's how I spent my retirement.

Financing my retirement

I am thankful to my Creator for giving me the means to kick start my planning to start saving for my retirement.

I started twenty years ago with something small and had gradually upped the monthly saving as my salary increased. Whatever extras received from other sources I'd save a percentage of it.

I wasn't following any rigid imposition to acquire maximum saving nor was I racing with time to achieve it. I was merely doing it consistently and had avoided using my other savings accounts.

In this way, more avenues of my other tangible assets remain during retirement. Within the three years of retirement, I've learnt how to gauge my well-being financially and spiritually for many years to come.

Always remember that saving is a good habit worth continuing even during your retirement. You don't need to have millions to retire. You simply need to make plans to live within your means. Put your money in a proper perspective and you're good to go.

Spiritual Needs

To me, spirituality is total submission of your will to your Creator. The more I learn about my faith, the more I learn about myself. I feel work has taken most of my time, leaving me behind in pursuing further knowledge to feed my soul.

While praying provides the solace you need, there is still much to be done for your emotional and spiritual health.

Since I've retired, I've had the time to attend lectures and enrol myself in a structured study programme. You always hear students dropping out of school but as for me, I'm proud to say that I've dropped in.

One of the reasons I'm going back to school in my later years is because I've been too busy with putting aside my earnings to the savings account, living expenses, my mother's monthly allowance and of course, some well-deserved luxury for myself.

My career may be over but never my quest for new knowledge. It's always been my goal to keep the mind active through learning. I'm also looking forward to socialising and connecting with people in a meaningful level. When I finally got the opportunity to pursue Islamic studies, I was one of the few mature students in the class. Despite the twenty or thirty year age difference, we get on really well with the younger students.

To say that you can't teach an old dog new tricks has proven to be an incorrect cliché. Mature students tend to do well because of their relevant life experience applied through the learning process. While we use our own funding to pursue further studies, juggling work and family have helped us to develop good organisational and time management skills.

As for me, I had to learn the hard way. But that's how it is in life; the things that are worth having are usually the ones we would have to work hard for.

Giving Depth to My Hobbies

The knowledge and skills you possess are your secret weapons in retirement. Take little steps at a time to nurture your passion. Keep the creativity alive and make it work for you.

Jewellery

I have been practicing, teaching and selling handmade jewellery on a small scale during my working years but have only started attending classes during retirement.

I've obtained a Diploma in Jewellery Arts together with several certificates for Gem Awareness, Professional Stringing, Professional Weaving, Professional Wirework and Art of Clay

Modelling. All of these, I do it in the name of creativity and my passion for jewellery.

Now I'm looking forward to putting my skills to the test and on to the next level. I'm certain this will result in the fruition of new perspectives and opportunities . . .

Arts and Crafts

Arts and Crafts have always been a source of relaxation for me. Every completed piece of artwork never fails to give me a sense of accomplishment. It's a process that inspires insight and a sense of awareness that could help with improving interpersonal skills.

For the past three years, I've taught Arts and Crafts to children as young as two years old. However it's been less teaching and more of a learning experience for me. Their many antics, while entertaining, have taught me to be more patient.

My adult students, mostly homemakers and retirees, have yet to master holding a brush. Oil and acrylic are something new and foreign to them. But as soon as they're able to overcome their fear, their creativity becomes unstoppable.

It's always a reward to see the smiles on my students' faces after completing their first masterpieces.

As for me, I work on oil and acrylic paintings at my own time and have sold a few pieces to local and international buyers.

I'm currently dabbling in cartooning as there are a lot of ideas I could draw from my own life experience.

Cooking and Baking

Every minute of your time is a learning process. After years of experiencing the hard knocks of life, learning something new has never been so much fun. I now try to look at things from different angles to gain new interests, new friends, a new sense of freedom and much more.

So for the past three years, I have managed to convert myself from zero to hero. I took up the challenge of pastry-making as one of the many series of baking and cooking lessons and have gone from not knowing to bake the simplest cookies to almost becoming a pastry chef with certificates to be proud of.

Coming from a financial work background, I thought then, hundreds and thousands are related to dollars and cents only. I learnt in my pastry class that there are also colourful little edible beadlets for cake decoration. In between the module courses, I jumped at every opportunity to attend crash courses.

Doing something out of love is doing it with great tenacity. So now every other day, I have freshly-made bread, cookies and pastries to enjoy at home.

There's more to life than just watching and getting your hands dirty to achieve results and perfection. You learn things by trial and error.

Don't let mistakes pull you down. Embrace it instead. Keep driving and maintain your focus. Winners will always want to do everything well no matter how trivial it is.

Photography

Photographs are like footprints of our past, frozen memories that we can hold in our hands.

My relationship with photography goes back a long way when I managed to exchange bubble gum cards for a camera. Having a camera was a luxury then. All the black and white photos of the late sixties and seventies in my family albums were taken by me.

I set aside time and some money to upgrade my skills from taking simple photo shoots to more technical shots, from film to cards and from SLR to DSLR.

To shoot eye-catching photos, you need to go through a learning process. And as always, practice makes perfect.

With years of travelling and tons of photographs, I am sure something tangible will come out from this.

Travelling

When I was growing up in a *kampung*, I used to keep newspapers with photos and news of foreign countries. It's actually the paper wrapping of vegetables that my mother bought from the market. This and together with my love for history fuelled my desire to see the world.

After ten years into my working life, I managed to start saving. Not only did I create a retirement account I also did a traveling account too.

After traveling the world half of my working life, I can proudly say that I have earned my degree for general knowledge about people and their way of life; the places, the food, the bad, the ugly and above all, the beauty in everything.

To me the world is like a book. If I do not travel, I read only a page.

Writing a Book

Even though I am an avid reader, it never crossed my mind that one day I'll be writing a book.

I've been toying with the idea since reaching the third year of my retirement. With time on my side, churning up a storyline is not a big problem for me. Plus there's so much I'm willing to share about my life experience.

However, finding a publisher could be a very daunting task. One should expect lots of rejections.

The big question is: Where do I begin and how? After getting some answers on the internet, I now have to prove myself that I can do this through self-publishing.

While considering this as an investment that I will not regret, I start writing about things that are close to my heart.

As you can see, retirement is just a beginning of a new life for me.

So far so good.

.........LEARNING SOMETHING NEW HAS NEVER BEEN SO
MUCH FUN.......A NEW SENSE OF FREEDOM

EXPANDING MY HORIZON

Taking my hobbies to the next level is something that I am planning to do next. After honing my skills for the last three years, now is the time to explore the many possibilities.

Earning an income from your hobby is one of the many possibilities and a nice way to get paid for doing something that you would do with pleasure. At times, you may find that bringing your hobbies to the next level may cause the joy steaming out of it. There is a balance to achieve. If you can find it, you can have fun while earning money on the side.

In order to earn some income, you need customers. I am fortunate that people around me know what I'm good at doing. It is a first start to marketing. Marketing through the internet has also made it possible for me to gain a wider customer base.

Here are some of the things I would like to see through into the next level. I'm slowly but surely working on making these projects happen:

Creating a Blog / Facebook page for:

- Selling hand-crafted jewellery
- Art workshops for both children and adults
- Selling my paintings and craft works
- Selling home-baked cookies for festive seasons
- Selling used novels, items to recycles etc

Writing a book

What possibilities can I achieve from my traveling? Stories of my travels and the many recipes from all over the world are a good combination for a cookbook or a travelogue.

I have been collating and kitchen testing my mother's recipes for quite awhile. It is time to get it compiled and published for the family's next generation.

My mother is a great source of information too. I have been audio taping her experiences during the Japanese occupation of Singapore during the period 1942 to 1945, something I would love to get published. I may use her experience as a backdrop of my first novel.

Also, I'd eventually like to write a book about hand-crafted jewellery.

I've been actively writing for a popular internet website through the IPad application called the Wattpad. This could be my launching pad for my writing venture and as a marketing avenue.

The possibilities to creativity, is endless. If we continue doing things the same way, we will definitely get the same results all the time. Why? because we failed to think out of the box. You just need time to discover your potential. The rest is not only history but also the future.

Studio and Home Office

Turning the extra room into a studio and a home office is next on the agenda. With minimal expenditure to go and a design to suit its multi-functionality, I want it to be an inspirational workspace.

I've been using it as an art studio where I paint and teach arts and crafts. It also functions as a guest and library room. With a few enhancements, I hope to create a conducive space for anyone using it.

While I am in no hurry to get it upgraded, it would be nice if I can get a sponsor to help me materialise my room makeover plans. I will find a way because I am good at it. Therefore, it is work in progress.

Voluntary work

Volunteering is second nature to me as I have been doing it since my youth days. Now that time is on my side, paying it forward seems like the natural thing to do.

There are many reasons why retirees take up voluntary work. Some see it as a way of contributing to society, while others see it as something that will enable them to have more contact with people and as an outlet for a meaningful commitment and self-satisfaction.

However, do not let voluntary work become a chore. Learn to say 'No' tactfully if you are needed to give more of your time. Limit your involvements if you have to.

As for me, I just want to make a difference.

I'm currently volunteering as an art teacher for children with special needs. I am also thinking of going back to school again to take up art therapy if time and financial needs permit it. I have also approach several voluntary organisations to offer my service. I am also involved in some special voluntary works overseas.

Whatever fields you choose to volunteer, you will find it rewarding and enriching your life in many ways. It is something that you will never regret doing.

Bonding Time

As you make new friends you should also strengthen your existing relationships with your old friends. Get connected with friends that you have lost touch with.

Ever wonder what's happened to some of your best friends from school? Your ex-colleagues, friends you have worked before when you were actively involved in clubs and associations?

Since my retirement I have managed to trace some of my old friends I have not been in touch with for quite sometime. I started having either tea, lunch or dinner with them for at least once a month. There is a lot of catching up to do. The search for old friends continues until this day.

My upcoming venture in keeping the friendship going is making sure everyone are contactable through social networking and planning activities together once in awhile.

We all need the friends we have, especially when we get older. The more friends we have, the better we tend to feel about ourselves.

I am happy to have a close-knit family. Family bonding time is a time spent together meaningfully. Striking the right balance between work and family is important.

In my family, Tuesday is set aside especially for my sisters who are homemakers. It is also potluck day. I used to miss this when I was working but have now been enjoying their company for the past three years. With me being the more active one, lots of activities such as doing arts and crafts and many more have been organised.

There are more activities in the making to keep the bonding even stronger; perhaps a family trip abroad or a grand family celebration.

Health Wellbeing

Getting old is unavoidable. We can't prevent it from happening but we can take measures to ensure that we get old by being fit, active and healthy. The effort you take now will make it easier in your later years because the older you get, the harder it gets to maintain an acceptable level of fitness.

Financial planning for retirement should also include financing for your medical needs because as we age our risks of getting major illness such as heart failure, diabetes and so on, increases. Our lifestyles play a major role in many of the conditions that commonly affect our quality of life as we get older.

To stay healthy long into your golden years makes the doctor your new best friend by visiting him or her regularly for medical check-ups and test.

Staying engaged with others by keeping active will definitely help to kill boredom and keep your mind sharp. These are just some of the factors that can keep your physical health in check.

Since my retirement, I have visited the doctor periodically for routine physical check-ups. So far so good, nothing major to worry about.

Always eat sensibly. Get your daily dose of fresh fruits and supplements to complement your diet. Keeping fit has become part of my routine for the past three years and is still continuing.

The sport stadium is just a walking distance from where I live. So every day, after my morning prayers, I will go there to do my Tai Chi, jogging and socialising.

To keep my mind sharp and agile, I do lots of brain exercises such as playing chess, Sudoku, reading, painting and so on.

Right now, I need to get a bicycle. This is the simplest of needs yet the hardest for me to fulfill.

Traveling

Seeing the world and experiencing different cultures can open our minds to new things and view life in exciting different ways. One important reason is that you discover a lot by learning to fend for yourself.

Besides providing a sense of adventure, it also opens doors to cultures other than yours. Sure you can get a coconut from the supermarket but nothing replaces the experience of getting it from the respective native lands.

You may discover that the biggest wood is not only in Hollywood but also in Bollywood, Kollywood, Malaywood . . .

Now that I've almost exhausted my traveling funds, I need to find ways to revitalise it:

After this book project, I may work on compiling a travel cookbook based on the countries I've visited. Perhaps this could help generate some passive income and contribute to my traveling funds.

How about giving motivational talks based on my travelling experiences to relevant groups?

Whether you travel to escape stress at work, or need time to contemplate where you are heading in life, or travel during your retirement, travelling seems to be the only valid answer.

However, keep an open mind. Travelling is a luxury and if you can afford it, you have to make the most out of it.

While we strive to achieve the best for ourselves, we often hit many walls. To pass through the walls, we have to stretch past the comfort zone. Most of the time, we try doing the wrong things correctly, and the right things wrongly.

It's the inevitable part of moving to the next level, where everything is worth trying.

FAMILY BONDING IS TIME SPENT TOGETHER MEANINGFULLY. STRIKING THE RIGHT BALANCE BETWEEN WORK AND FAMILY IS IMPORTANT

WE ALL NEED THE FRIENDS WE HAVE, ESPECIALLY WHEN WE
GET OLDER. THE MORE FRIENDS WE HAVE, THE BETTER WE
TEND TO FEEL ABOUT OURSELVES

WHAT OTHERS SAY ABOUT RETIREMENT

A chance to spend more time with family and friends, take up new hobbies and maybe travel the world.

Time to take stock. Ceasing employment is leaving the same office for good but entering the world with full of possibilities.

I would like very much to pack my bag and go. No more a slave of the alarm clock. So many choices and so much time. I just need to pursue them with open mind.

Jodie Nair, customer relation

Retirement is a time when your needs and wants become one.

The golden age-where one stops looking at the greener pastures on the other sides and starts reaping the gold in one's own backyard

When the tyres of a car become worn out, the car just needs to change them. I think the same goes for us. Growing older does not mean we become obsolete. We simply need to revisit our goals in life for us to start living again.

Norliza Mohd Ali, teacher

When I ceased employment I ceased to be indispensable for the office. When I retired my time becomes indispensable for me.

Goodbye tension, goodbye stress. Hello passion, hello rest.

I want my retirement to be a happy one full of enthusiasm, sound financial support for as long as I live, healthy and thankful.

Richard Chiam, retiree

To retire means breaking free from the rat race and being able to experience life to the fullest.

Work with what you've got.

I would like someday experience financial independence and give as much as I can to charity and good deeds; I would like to be the best person/soul that I can be in God's eyes and live life as passionately, creatively and meaningfully as possible.

Nadia Adi, entrepreneur

Rest and relax and do things within my own pace without a need to meet dateline.

Take one day at a time and not to worry about the future.

To devout more time to Allah.

Khalthum Abu Talib, tax officer

After years of hard work I deserved a good rest. and reaping whatever I've sow. That's what retirement is for me.

It's hard work going up a hill but a breeze descending it, but do take care as there are still little obstacles along the way down.

Spending more quality time with my family. Being there always and to see the world.

T.T.Tan, retiree

Retirement is when you stop lying about your age and start telling the truth to earn the many discounts and privileges for seniors.

Spend wisely because money don't come easy.

Writing a book is foremost on my mind. With retirement I hope to achieve my dream and put down my experiences on paper.

Ben Justin, financial manager

—∘∘∙◉∙∘∘—

To me retirement means entering another phase of life. Finally able to relinquish the roles and freed of the responsibilities at work. To be able to spend more quality time with loved ones, including close friends and oneself. Living life at a slower pace and taking time to sip a cuppa and smell some flowers.

Live, Love and Laugh!

Perhaps one more . . . . Slow and steady goes a long way . . .

Serene Tay, tax officer

TO ME THE WORLD IS LIKE A BOOK. IF I DO NOT TRAVEL, I
READ ONLY A PAGE

......IT'S BEEN LESS TEACHING AND MORE OF A LEARNING
EXPERIENCE FOR ME. THEIR MANY ANTICS, WHILE
ENTERTAINING, HAVE TAUGHT ME TO BE MORE PATIENT

CREATIVITY IN RETIREMENT

I never had a hobby and don't know what else to do besides going through my routined lifestyle. On my off days, I usually play with my grandchildren, read papers, watch television . . . . I am not good with my hands . . . . I am worried that I will be bored to death in my retirement.

Sounds familiar? So you think you don't belong to the creative lots? Even before you embark on your creativity journey, your innermost thoughts will lash at you "creativity cannot be taught!'

Well, there's no right or wrong answer to it. It's like nature and nurture complementing each other.

Being creative or artistic doesn't mean in terms of physical actions only. It is also a way of thinking, a way of doing and viewing things.

To think creative, first we need to eradicate the usual thinking patterns. Continuing doing the same thing the same way will get you the same result. If you don't mind the same result then it's okay. What if you want a 'wow' result? Think out of the box, which is simply to think differently, unconventionally or from a new perspective. In retirement I had the opportunity to experiment with lateral thinking. Trials and errors on many interests keep me in check. Sometime routine can also be positive if you can develop 'creative rituals' that enable you to have a creative mindset.

Children learnt by copying from the adults around them. As they grow up they learn to develop own ways and thus transcending beyond what is known to them. As adults we can still learn by copying. When I first started to paint I learned, studied and copied from various artists. Soon I develop my own style. Same goes for writing. I was never good at writing because I never tried hard enough. So when the urge to write a book suddenly triggered that right hemisphere, I take action. Not only did I read many novels but I studied styles, storyline and so on. I opened myself to possibility and watched the process unfold. If you wait for inspiration to write, than you are not a writer, you are a waiter. Just write, slowly but surely ideas will flow naturally.

Other possibility to develop a creative mindset is to get involve in circles of creative people. I am lucky that I constantly meet creative people be it my art students, the volunteers I work with, friends around me or those close to me. I believe that nobody is born without creative tendencies and abilities. Some people are good at putting their ideas across while others need a little push. Insight without action is useless and creativity without confidence is as good as back to square one.

Nowadays whenever I leave home there are two things that I will always have in my carrier. Never leave home without it. No, I am not talking about credit cards. Yes a notebook and a pen to jot down ideas because you never know when the brainwave going to strike.

Do you know when will you be at your most or least creative? Try to identify and make the most use of it to your advantage. Mine strike at the time when I am most relaxed and normally during bedtime. I can create stories and think of better ways to do my daytime projects while I am counting the sheep.

Like other parts of the body, brain too need regular exercise to stay sharp, focus and agile. I spend my downtime doing crossword puzzles, soduku, chess and engaged in computer games.

Experience something new once in a while to expand your creative horizon.

LAST BUT NOT LEAST

Regardless whether you are working, contemplating or well into your retirement the change is still a challenging life transition. Making changes in your lifestyle is not an easy one. However, take little steps at a time to make it work for you.

Money is always a big issue but that do not mean you are going to have a hard time during retirement. Your primary goal every month is to spend less than what you bring in or planned. Doing it consistently will ease your financial situation. Accumulate inspirations around you because you need it to make your retirement the best time of your life. Get motivated by it, be creative and most important to have a positive view of your retirement.

Select enjoyable and meaningful activities that allow you to get by with the money you have included in your planning. This is also the time you do lots of testing, experimenting, implementing your dreams, your wants, needs and your options that make for a better life. From here you will also learn to adjust according to the situation that works best for you.

Hopefully you have learnt a thing or two from this book about how I spent three years of retirement living simply and happily even not having millions to sit on. The journey still continue regardless whether there are stumbling blocks along the way which I will treat it as stepping stones for a better path ahead. So far so good.

Thank you for reading this book. I hope you will enjoy reading it as much as I enjoyed sharing it with you.

Mariati Yahya

I HAVE BEEN COLLATING AND KITCHEN TESTING MY MOTHER'S RECIPES FOR QUITE AWHILE. IT IS TIME TO COMPILE AND PUBLISHED FOR THE FAMILY'S NEXT GENERATION

WHILE WE STRIVE TO ACHIEVE THE BEST FOR OURSELVES, WE OFTEN HIT MANY WALLS. TO PASS THROUGH THE WALLS, WE HAVE TO STRETCH BEYOND THE COMFORT ZONE

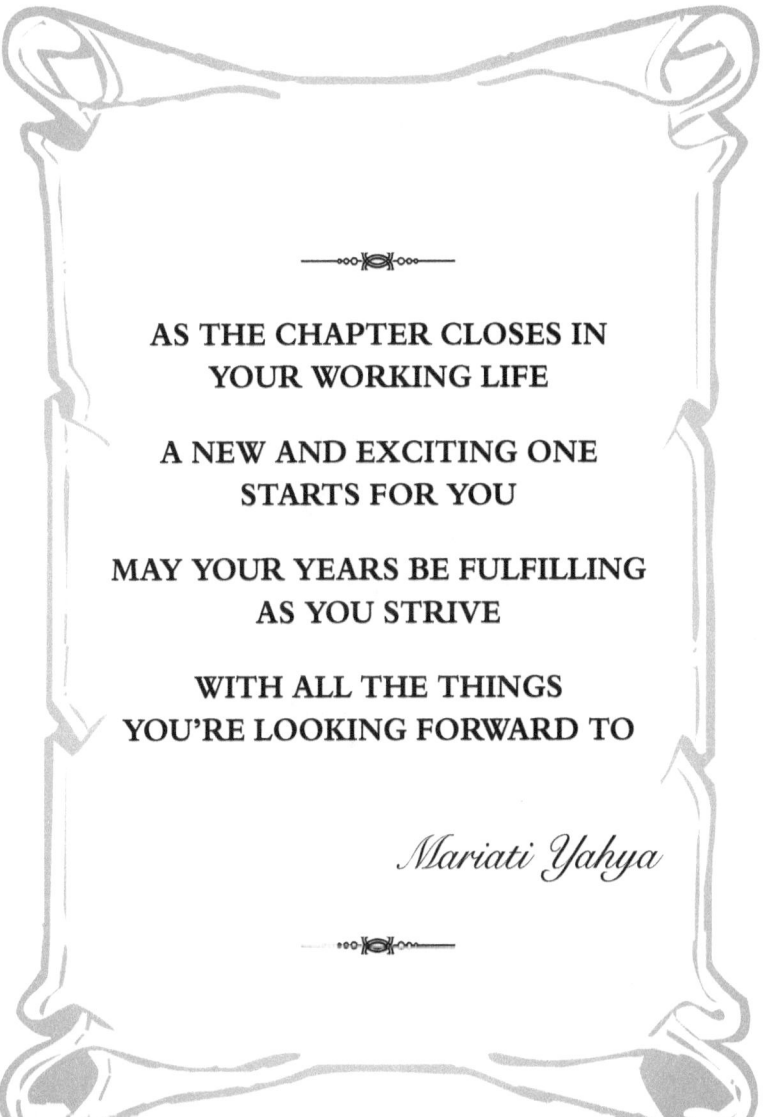

AS THE CHAPTER CLOSES IN
YOUR WORKING LIFE

A NEW AND EXCITING ONE
STARTS FOR YOU

MAY YOUR YEARS BE FULFILLING
AS YOU STRIVE

WITH ALL THE THINGS
YOU'RE LOOKING FORWARD TO

Mariati Yahya